Future SmartMinds

Future ✚ ━ ✖ ➗ ━ Mathematician

www.futuresmartminds.com

Welcome to the **FutureSmartMinds** family!

Thank you for choosing "**Future Mathematician**". Your support means the world to us as we strive to develop young minds in STEM (Science, Technology, Engineering, and Mathematics) skills. We believe that learning should be engaging and fun, and "**Future Mathematician**" is designed to make math an exciting adventure for young learners.

Your feedback is incredibly valuable to us. If you have a moment, please consider sharing your thoughts and rating us on Amazon. Your input not only helps us improve but also guides other parents and educators in their quest for high-quality STEM resources.

Scan to Rate Us on Amazon

Thank you for your trust in **FutureSmartMinds**. Together, we're nurturing future mathematicians and fostering a love for learning in the minds of tomorrow. Happy learning!

Warm regards,

The **FutureSmartMinds** Team

www.futuresmartminds.com

Email: FutureSmartMindsKids@gmail.com

 @futuresmartminds

 @futuresmartminds

 @ futuresmartminds

Scan to visit our website

Content	Page
What is Mathematics?	4
Mathematics Timeline	5
(1) Fractions Made Fun • Comparing fractions • Adding and subtracting fractions	8
Mental workout Help Eldon buy pizza!	12
(2) Whole Numbers Adventure • Rounding decimals to the nearest whole number • Rounding fractions to the nearest whole number	18
Mental workout Help Kayla win a movie ticket!	20
(3) Percentage Explorations • Turning a percentage into a decimal • Turning a fraction into a percentage • Finding a percentage of an amount • Rates and percentages	24
Mental workout Eldon in the shopping mall!	28
(4) Pie Charts Discovery	32
Mental workout Popcorn flavour preferences!	34
(5) Budgeting Basics • Income • Needs and wants • Saving goals • The 50/30/20 rule	38

What is Mathematics?

The great philosopher **Galileo** once said: "To understand the universe, you must understand the language in which it is written, the language of Mathematics". Just like the English language, Mathematics allows people to communicate with each other, conduct trades, build structures, develop technologies, and understand how the universe functions.

You are surrounded by math, from simple daily life planning to plants' shapes and atoms' structures. You use math to communicate essential information, such as age, time, and distance.

Math is essential for all professions: for **engineers** to build infrastructures and solve problems, for **teachers** to plan for their classes, for **doctors** to prescribe medicine doses, for **pilots** to navigate, and for **scientists** and researchers to prove their theories.

Math is vital for **creative thinking**, **problem-solving**, and **logical reasoning**. Our modern civilization, cities, homes, telecommunication, industries, and transportation were developed because of advances in math. Mathematical thinking builds your mind and helps you develop the skills necessary to imagine and design for the future.

Mathematics Timeline

The origin of **mathematics** goes back to prehistoric times when humans used bone checkmarks to count. The earliest mathematical texts available came from Mesopotamia (Iraq) around 3000 BC. **Babylonian mathematics**, written by the people of Mesopotamia, was mainly concerned with financial counting, including grain allotments and weights of minerals and liquids.

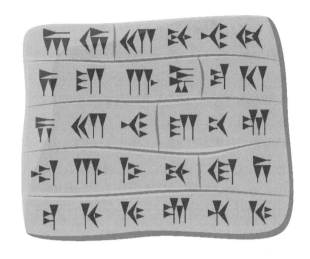

Babylonian mathematics used a **sexagesimal numeral system** which uses 60 as its base. This system is still used nowadays in measuring time, such as 60 seconds in a minute and 60 minutes in an hour.

An instruction manual for students in arithmetic and geometry, called **Rhind Papyrus**, was written in 1650 BC by the **Egyptians**. This manual presented area formulas, methods for multiplication and division, and unit fractions.

Inspired by Babylonian and Egyptian mathematics, **Greek mathematics** used logic to derive conclusions and mathematical rigour (constraints) to prove them. **Thales of Miletus** (~600 BC) is considered the first true mathematician to apply deductive reasoning to geometry. The study of mathematics as an independent subject began when **Pythagoras** (~550 BC) established the first school of mathematics with the motto "**All is Number**". The Pythagoreans came up with the first proof of the Pythagorean theorem, which presented the relationships between the three sides of a right triangle.

Julius Caesar (~100 BC) replaced the early Roman lunar calendar with a solar one, called the **Julian calendar**, which consisted of 365 days yearly with an additional leap day every fourth year. An error of 11 minutes and 14 seconds in the Julian calendar was corrected in the 15th century. We use the corrected calendar now as the international standard calendar.

In the 7th century, **Brahmagupta** from India explained zero as a placeholder and decimal digit and the Hindu-Arabic numeral system. **Islamic mathematicians** adapted this numeral system and introduced it to Europe by the 12th century. The **Arabic numeral system**, which we use nowadays, has replaced all older number systems across the world.

The Islamic empire (the Middle East, Central Asia, North Africa, Iberia, and parts of India) made considerable contributions towards advancing modern mathematics. **Al-Khwarizmi** wrote two critical books in the 8th century on the Hindu-Arabic numerals and methods of solving equations.

Al-Khwarizmi is described as the **father of algebra** since he was the first to solve equations using reduction and balancing methods. The term algebra came from his book "**Al-Jaber**", an Arabic word meaning "completion"; the term **algorithm** came from his name. Translation of his books in the 12th century introduced principal mathematics to the Western world.

In the 17th century, Europe led the advances in science and mathematics. For example, **Galileo** used a telescope to observe the moons of Jupiter. His ideas allowed for gathering mathematical data describing the positions of the planets. **Isaac Newton** discovered the laws of physics and created the concept of **calculus**. **Leibniz** developed the calculus notion and refined the binary system used in all digital computers.

The 19th century saw the beginning of abstract algebra and group theory. In the 20th and 21st centuries, mathematics became a significant profession. Computers improved from analog to digital machines, allowing for industrial revolution. New areas of mathematics evolved, such as information technology, signal processing, data analysis, and optimization.

The advances in mathematical knowledge have led to specialization. Currently, hundreds of mathematical subjects are being studied in schools and colleges. Hundreds of journals are specialized in publishing new research from around the world. You must develop your mathematical skills and gain the core knowledge needed for your studies and future profession. Think about mathematics as an enjoyable mental game that you need to excel to participate in building our future!

(1) Fractions Made Fun

A fraction represents a part of a whole. When you break down a whole unit, a fraction shows how many pieces you have from the whole. It is expressed as the number of equal pieces over one whole piece. When writing a fraction, there are two main parts: the top is the numerator, and the bottom is the denominator.

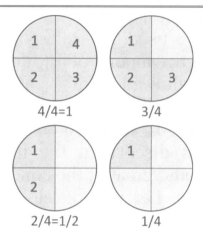

$$\frac{\textbf{Numerator}}{\textbf{Denominator}} = \frac{\text{(How many parts you have)}}{\text{(How many parts the whole was divided into)}}$$

Comparing fractions

Sometimes we need to compare fractions to determine which is bigger or smaller. It is easy to compare two fractions when they have the same denominator by looking at the numerator, for example:

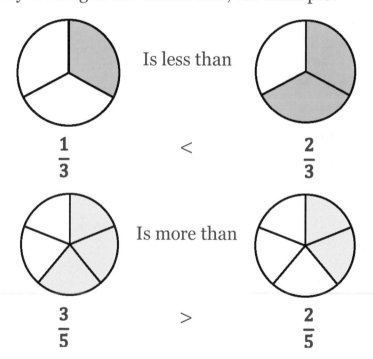

However, when the two fractions do not have the same denominator, we need to find the Least Common Multiple (LCM) that makes the denominators the same to compare them. The LCM of two numbers can be found by listing their multiples and selecting the smallest common multiple, as illustrated in the following example:

Example

To find the Least Common Multiple of 3 and 4, we list the first few multiples for both numbers:

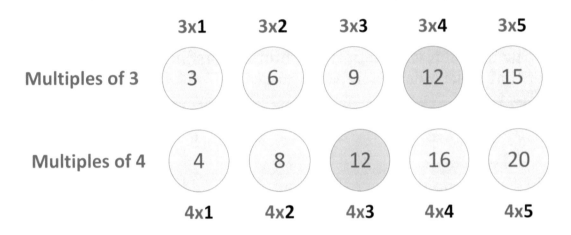

We can see that 12 is the smallest multiple which is common between the multiples of 3 and 4. Therefore the LCM of 3 and 4 is 12.

To compare two fractions with different denominators, we need to find the LCM of the denominators and multiply both the numerator and denominator with that multiple.

Sometimes, finding the LCM is not easy, especially when the denominators are large. In this case, multiplying the denominators is the easiest way to find a common denominator. This method returns a common denominator, which could be the least common denominator or could be not. However, it is still a helpful method for comparing fractions.

Example

Determine which fraction is bigger from the following fractions:

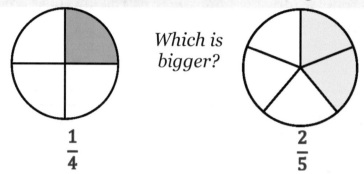

$$\frac{1}{4}$$

Which is bigger?

$$\frac{2}{5}$$

First, we need to find the LCM of the denominators. In this case, the LCM of 4 and 5 is 20. Then we multiply the numerators and denominators by the number that makes the denominator 20:

$$\frac{1}{4} = \frac{1 \times 5}{4 \times 5} = \frac{5}{20} \qquad\qquad \frac{2}{5} = \frac{2 \times 4}{5 \times 4} = \frac{8}{20}$$

Now, we can compare the two fractions $^5/_{20}$ and $^8/_{20}$ since they have the same denominator. Since $5 < 8$, then $^5/_{20} < {}^8/_{20}$.

Therefore, $^1/_4 < {}^2/_5$.

In this example, the common denominator obtained by multiplying the denominators ($4 \times 5 = 20$) is the least common denominator.

Adding and subtracting fractions

Adding and subtracting fractions helps you handle situations where things are divided into parts. For example, when you share a chocolate bar with your friend, if each of you ate only a part of it, you will need to add the fractions to figure out how much of the bar was eaten.

Adding and subtracting fractions with the same denominators is straightforward. When the denominators are the same, we add or subtract the numerators, which will become the resulting numerator, whereas the denominator stays the same. However, when we add or subtract fractions with different denominators, we need to find the least common denominator and multiply the numerator with the number that results in the least common multiplier before we add or subtract the numerators.

Example

Let's add $^1/_5$ and $^4/_5$, since the fractions have the same denominators, we add the numerators as follows:

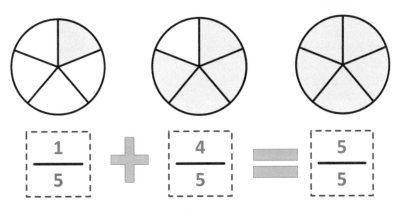

Now, let's add $^1/_5$ and $^2/_6$, since the fractions have different denominators, we need to find the LCM of the denominators. In this case, the LCM of 5 and 6 is 30. Then, we multiply the numerators and denominators by the number that makes the denominator 30.

Once the denominators have a common value, which is 30 in this example, we can add the fractions by adding the numerators.

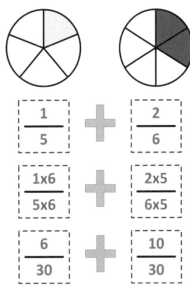

Mental workout

Help Eldon buy pizza!

Eldon decided to treat himself to Pizza after he completed his mental workout, which consisted of awesome, enjoyable, and mind-blowing math activities (similar to the mental workout activities you will enjoy throughout this book!). Help Eldon select a bigger Pizza portion for the money he has from the following offers:

Example

If Eldon has $2, which offer should he select to get a bigger Pizza portion?

$$\boxed{A} \quad or \quad \boxed{B}$$

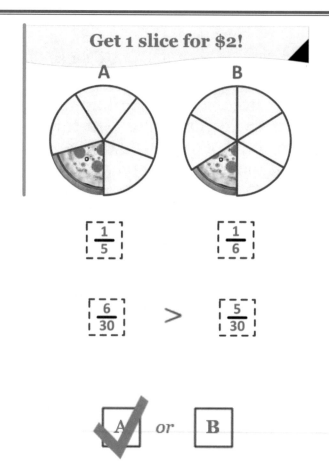

Get 1 slice for $2!

A   B

Step1: write the fraction representing the portion of Pizza offered

$$\frac{1}{5} \qquad \frac{1}{6}$$

Step 2: find the equivalent fractions with common denominators and compare them

$$\frac{6}{30} \quad > \quad \frac{5}{30}$$

Step 3: select the bigger portion of the Pizza

$$\boxed{A} ✓ \quad or \quad \boxed{B}$$

MW1.1: If Eldon has $2, which offer should he select to get a bigger Pizza portion?

[A] or [B]

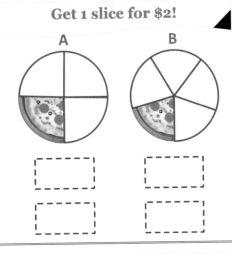

MW1.2: If Eldon has $3, which offer should he select to get a bigger Pizza portion?

[A] or [B]

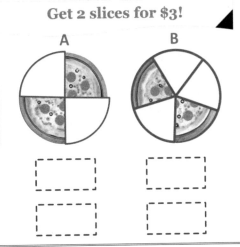

MW1.3: If Eldon has $4, which offer should he select to get a bigger Pizza portion?

[A] or [B]

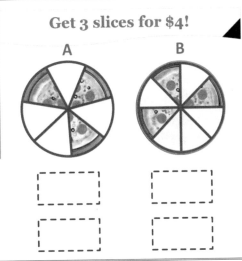

Future➕➖✖➗ Mathematician   13

MW1.4: If Eldon has $4, which offer should he select to get a bigger Pizza portion?

A *or* B

Get 3 slices for $4!
A

Get 5 slices for $4!
B

MW1.5: If Eldon has $6, which offer should he select to get a bigger Pizza portion?

A *or* B

Get 5 slices for $6!
A

Get 4 slices for $6!
B

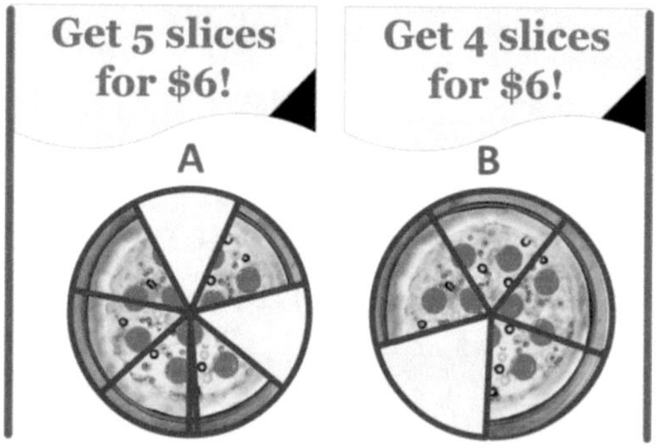

MW1.6: If Eldon has $8, which offer should he select to get a bigger Pizza portion?

A *or* B

Get 6 slices for $8!
A

Get 5 slices for $8!
B

After using his fractional skills, Eldon ended up getting 5 slices of his favourite Pizza for $4. However, fractions keep coming up to Eldon in everyday situations. Going back home, he must decide which road saves him time. Help Eldon taking the shortest path home!

MW1.7: which road should Eldon take to save time on his way back home?

A   or   B

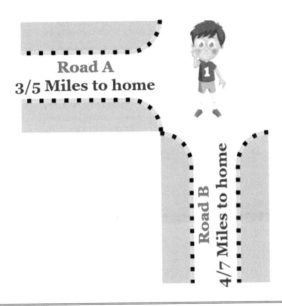

MW1.8: which road should Eldon take to save time on his way back home?

A   or   B

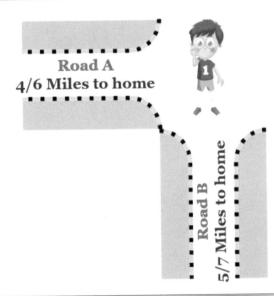

(2) Whole Numbers Adventure

A whole number is a positive number that does not include a fractional or decimal part. These numbers are also called integers. For example, Numbers like 0,1,2,3, 11, and 101 are whole numbers, whereas numbers like -3, -1, 3.7, and $3\frac{1}{7}$ are not whole numbers.

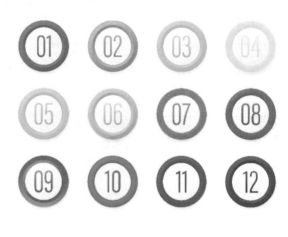

Rounding decimals to the nearest whole number

Rounding decimals to the nearest whole number converts an exact value into a whole number that is easier to remember and use. For example, if you need 7.81 minutes to finish a math activity, you could express the time required for the activity as 8 minutes, using the nearest whole number. Rounding can be used when the exact value is not needed, and an approximate value serves the purpose.

Example

Exact value	Nearest whole number value	Method
3.25	3	To round a decimal number, check the 10th digit, the first digit to the right of the decimal point. The exact value is rounded down if the 10th digit is less than 5. The exact value is rounded up if the value is more than or equal to 5.
3.50	4	
3.75	4	

Rounding fractions to the nearest whole number

There are three different types of fractions that you can identify by looking at the numerator and denominator:

Fraction type	Criteria	Examples			
Proper fraction	The numerator is less than the denominator.	$\dfrac{1}{2}$	$\dfrac{1}{4}$	$\dfrac{11}{15}$	$\dfrac{19}{27}$
Improper fraction	The numerator is greater than the denominator.	$\dfrac{3}{2}$	$\dfrac{9}{5}$	$\dfrac{15}{7}$	$\dfrac{23}{19}$
Mixed fraction	The fraction has a whole number part and a fractional part.	$1\dfrac{1}{2}$	$3\dfrac{2}{5}$	$2\dfrac{3}{7}$	$5\dfrac{5}{7}$

When you round **proper fractions** to the nearest whole number, the fraction is compared with $1/2$. The given fraction is rounded down if it is less than $1/2$ or rounded up if it is more than or equals to $1/2$.

Example

Suppose that you cut a whole pizza into 5 slices. You ate 2 slices and want to give your friend the remaining 3 slices. That is, you want to give your friend $3/5$ of the whole pizzza.

To round the proper fraction $3/5$ to the nearest whole number, we compare $3/5$ with $1/2$. To do that, the fractions must have a common denominator. Using the LCM method, we find that the equivalent to $3/5$ is $6/10$ and the equivalent to $1/2$ is $5/10$.

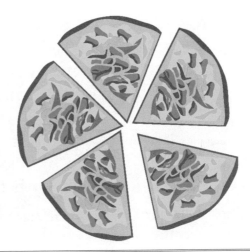

Now we can compare $^6/_{10}$ with $^5/_{10}$ as follows:

$$^6/_{10} > {}^5/_{10} \Rightarrow {}^3/_5 > {}^1/_2$$

Since $^3/_5$ is bigger than $^1/_2$, we should round up $^3/_5$ to the nearest whole number, which is **1**.

When we round **mixed fractions**, we leave the whole number part aside and compare the fractional part with $^1/_2$. The fractional part is rounded down if it is less than $^1/_2$ or rounded up if it is more than or equals to $^1/_2$.

Example

Suppose that you have 3 ice cream bars. You ate $1/4^{\text{th}}$ of one bar; the remaining is $2\,^3/_4$. The remaining is a mixed fraction, which we could round to the nearest whole number, as follows:

To round $2\,^3/_4$ to the nearest whole number, we look at the fractional part $^3/_4$ and compare it with $^1/_2$. The fractions must have a common denominator to compare them. Using the LCM method, we find that the equivalent to $^3/_4$ is still $^3/_4$ and the equivalent to $^1/_2$ is $^2/_4$. Now we can see that $^3/_4 > {}^2/_4$. Hence, $^3/_4 > {}^1/_2$.

Since the fractional part $^3/_4$ is bigger than $^1/_2$, we should round up the mixed fraction $2\,^3/_4$ to the nearest whole number, which is **3**.

When we round an **improper fraction**, we convert it into a **mixed fraction**. We leave the whole number part aside and compare the fractional part with $1/2$. The fractional part is rounded down if it is less than $1/2$ or rounded up if it is more than or equals to $1/2$.

Example

Let's take the improper fraction $9/4$. It means that you have 9 parts out of 4. We could round it to the nearest whole number as follows:

Step1: convert the improper fraction into a mixed fraction

When we divide 9 by 4 we get 2 as the quotient and 1 as the remainder. Therefore, the improper fraction $9/4$ is equivalent to the mixed fraction $2\,1/4$.

$$9/4 \qquad\qquad 2\,1/4$$

Improper fraction   **Mixed fraction**

Step2: round the mixed fraction to the nearest whole number

To round $2\,1/4$ to the nearest whole number, we look at the fractional part $1/4$ and compare it with $1/2$. The fractions must have a common denominator to compare them. Using the LCM method, we find that the equivalent to $1/4$ is still $1/4$ and the equivalent to $1/2$ is $2/4$. Now we can see that $1/4 < 2/4$. Hence, $1/4 < 1/2$.

Since the fractional part $1/4$ is less than $1/2$, we should round down the mixed fraction $2\,1/4$ to the nearest whole number, which is 2.

Hence, the improper fraction $9/4$ is rounds to the nearest whole number 2.

Mental workout

Help Kayla win a movie ticket!

Kayla did not realize how important her skills in fractions are until she visited the zoo. When she arrived, she was surprised that it offered a free movie ticket to the latest movie for anyone who could spot 2/3rd of the monkeys holding bananas from their monkey groups. Kayla took several rounds in the zoo to spot monkeys with bananas to be the lucky winner. Help Kayla win the movie ticket!

Example

In one of her rounds in the zoo, Kayla could see a group of monkeys. What is the fraction of monkeys with bananas in this group?

	Fraction of monkeys with bananas	Winning fraction
Step 1: find the fraction of monkeys with bananas	$\dfrac{2}{7}$	$\dfrac{2}{3}$
Step 2: Find the LCM	$\dfrac{2 \times 3}{7 \times 3}$	$\dfrac{2 \times 7}{3 \times 7}$
Step 3: Compare the fractions	$\dfrac{6}{21}$ <	$\dfrac{14}{21}$

Did Kayla win the movie ticket in this round?

Y *or*

MW2.1: In her first round in the zoo, Kayla could see a group of monkeys. What is the fraction of monkeys with bananas in this group?

	Fraction of monkeys with bananas	Winning fraction
Step1: find the fraction of monkeys with bananas	_____	$\frac{2}{3}$
Step 2: Find the LCM	_____	_____
Step 3: Compare the fractions	_____	_____

Did Kayla win the movie ticket in this round?

Y   or   N

MW2.2: In her second round in the zoo, Kayla could see a group of monkeys. What is the fraction of monkeys with bananas in this group?

	Fraction of monkeys with bananas	Winning fraction
Step1: find the fraction of monkeys with bananas	_____	$\frac{2}{3}$
Step 2: Find the LCM	_____	_____
Step 3: Compare the fractions	_____	_____

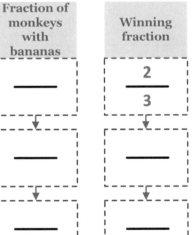

Did Kayla win the movie ticket in this round?

Y   or   N

MW2.3: In her third round in the zoo, Kayla could see a group of monkeys. What is the fraction of monkeys with bananas in this group?

	Fraction of monkeys with bananas	Winning fraction
Step1: find the fraction of monkeys with bananas	_____	$\dfrac{2}{3}$
Step 2: Find the LCM	_____	_____
Step 3: Compare the fractions	_____	_____

Did Kayla win the movie ticket in this round?

Y   or   N

MW2.4: In her fourth round in the zoo, Kayla could see a group of monkeys. What is the fraction of monkeys with bananas in this group?

	Fraction of monkeys with bananas	Winning fraction
Step1: find the fraction of monkeys with bananas	_____	$\dfrac{2}{3}$
Step 2: Find the LCM	_____	_____
Step 3: Compare the fractions	_____	_____

Did Kayla win the movie ticket in this round?

Y   or   N

MW2.5: In her fifth round in the zoo, Kayla could see a monkey group. What is the fraction of monkeys with bananas in this group?

Fraction of monkeys with bananas	Winning fraction
Step1: find the fraction of monkeys with bananas _____	$\frac{2}{3}$
Step 2: Find the LCM _____	_____
Step 3: Compare the fractions _____	_____

Did Kayla win the movie ticket in this round?

Y or N

MW2.6: Kayla ended up winning one movie tickets on her trip to the zoo. Could you figure out which round was the lucky round for Kayla?

MW2.1	MW2.2	MW2.3	MW2.4	MW2.5
1st round	2nd round	3rd round	4th round	5th round

(**Hint**: compare the results from MW2.1 to MW2.5 with the winning fraction $\frac{2}{3}$. Kayla must have seen fractions of monkeys with bananas bigger than $\frac{2}{3}$ in her winning round.)

(3) Percentage Explorations

A percentage is a number that expresses a fraction out of 100, followed by a percent sign (%). Just like when you cut a whole Pizza into 100 slices, each slice represents 1/100 or 1% of the entire Pizza. You see percentages in everyday life, like "10% off" at a store, which means you save $10 out of every $100.

Turning a percentage into a decimal

Think of the percentage as a fraction. "Percent" means "per hundred", so when you see 25%, it means 25/100. Dividing by 100 is the same as multiplying by 0.01. Therefore, to turn any percentage into a decimal, add a decimal point by the end of the number if it was not there, then move it two digits to the left and remove the percentage sign, as follows:

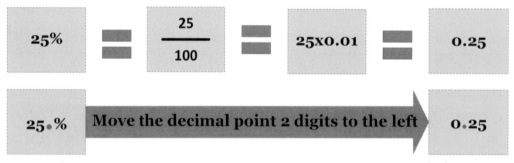

When you move the decimal point two digits, you change the fraction from parts out of 100 to parts out of 1. For example, 50% is the same as 0.50, 35% is the same as 0.35, and 40.5% is the same as 0.405. The decimal form allows you to use simple math operations, like multiplication and division, to find the answers.

Turning a fraction into a percentage

Percentages are used a lot in everyday life. You see them in shops, banks, and statistics. When you turn a fraction into a percentage, it helps you communicate your ideas clearly. For example, if you got 9 out of 10 questions right in a test, it is easier to say you got 90%. It is easier for a shop to offer a 10% discount instead of saying $10 off for every $100 you spend. To convert a fraction into a percentage, you first need to convert the fraction into a decimal and then convert the decimal into a percentage.

Example

Suppose you have a basket of fruits with 4 bananas, 3 apples, and 1 pear. What is the percentage of each type of fruit in the basket?

Step1: Find the total number of fruits.

First, we need to add together the different types of fruits to get the total number:

$$4 \text{ bananas} + 3 \text{ apples} + 1 \text{ pear} = 8 \text{ fruits}$$

Step2: Find the fraction of each type of fruits.

Each type of fruit is represented as a fraction using the total number of fruits as a denominator.

Step3: Convert the fractions into decimals.

Step3: Multiple the decimals by 100% to get the percentages.

When multiplying by 100%, we move the digital point two digits to the right and add the percentage sign.

Fruit type	Fraction	Decimal	Percentage
Bananas	$\dfrac{4}{8}$	0.50	$0.50 \times 100\% = 50\%$
Apples	$\dfrac{3}{8}$	0.375	$0.375 \times 100\% = 37.5\%$
Pears	$\dfrac{1}{8}$	0.125	$0.125 \times 100\% = 12.5\%$
Total	$\dfrac{8}{8} = 1$	**1**	**100%**

Therefore, the basket consists of 50% bananas, 37.5% apples, and 12.5% pears. The sum of these percentages must be 100%.

Finding a percentage of an amount

Now that you know how to turn a percentage into a decimal, it will be easy to find a percentage of an amount. Let's look at an example where you see a price tag with an offered discount:

Example

A retail shop offers a sale of 30% on pants. If the pant's original price was $50, what would be the price after the sale?

Step1: Convert the percentage into decimal

To convert a percentage into a decimal, we divide by 100. That is we move the decimal point two digits to the left.

$$30\% = \frac{30}{100} = 0.30$$

Step2: Multiply the decimal by the original amount

$$\textbf{Discount} = \mathbf{0.30 \times \$50 = \$15}$$

This means that $15 discount is offered from the original $50 price. The discount amount unit ($) is the same as the original amount unit.

Step3: Remove the discount amount from the original price

$$\textbf{Price after discount} = \mathbf{\$50 - \$15 = \$35}$$

The price of the pants after discount will be **$35**.

Alternative method

We can calculate the remianing percentage after removing the discount, that is 100% − 30% = 70% = 0.70. This remianing percentage means that the price after discount is 70% of the original price. The price after discount can be calculated by multiplying the remaining percentage by the original price:

$$\textit{Price after discount} = \mathbf{0.70 \times \$50 = \$35}$$

Rates and percentages

A rate is a ratio between two quantities. For example, if you ride your bike for 12 miles in 2 hours, the rate is the miles you drove divided by the hours. In this case, the rate represents two quantities: miles and hours. This rate is known as speed, which shows how fast or slow your ride was.

$$\text{Speed 1} = \frac{12\ miles}{2\ hours} = 6\ ^{mile}/_{hour} = 6\ MPH$$

Rates are usually compared using percentages. For example, if the same bike ride of 12 miles took you 1.8 hours instead of 2 hours, your new speed is calculated as:

$$\text{Speed 2} = \frac{12\ miles}{1.8\ hours} = 6.67\ ^{mile}/_{hour} = 6.67\ MPH$$

You could compare your first and second speeds using percentages to track the improvements in your rides by dividing the new rate by the original one and multiplying by 100%:

$$\text{Percentage change in speed} = \frac{\text{Speed 2}}{\text{Speed 1}} \times 100\% = \frac{6.67\ \text{MPH}}{6.00\ \text{MPH}} \times 100\%$$

$$= 1.11 \times 100\% = 111\%$$

Therefore, your second ride was 111% faster than your first ride. That is, your speed has increased by 11%. On the contrary, if a third ride of the same 12 miles took you 2.2 hours, your new rate is calculated as:

$$\text{Speed 3} = \frac{12\ \text{miles}}{2.2\ \text{hours}} = 5.45\ ^{mile}/_{hour} = 5.45\ \text{MPH}$$

$$\text{Percentage change in speed} = \frac{\text{Speed 3}}{\text{Speed 1}} \times 100\% = \frac{5.45\ \text{MPH}}{6.00\ \text{MPH}} \times 100\%$$

$$= 0.90 \times 100\% = 90\%$$

Therefore, your third ride was 90% slower than your first ride. That is, your speed has decreased by 10%.

Mental workout

Eldon in the shopping mall!

Eldon saved $150 for the day the shopping mall went on sale. He grabbed his shopping bag and went to the mall. Most shops offered a discount of up to 50% of their original price. He must find the best deals to get all he wants without exceeding his $150. Help Eldon keep track of his budget by finding the discounted price and the percentage it represents from his total money!

Example

Eldon bought a backpack from a shop that offered a discount of 30%. If the original price was $50, what is the price after the discount, and what is its percentage from the $150 that Eldon has?

Discount (% into decimal)	30% = 0.30
Discount amount ($)	$= 0.30 \times \$50 = \$15$
Price after discount ($)	$= \$50 - \$15 = \$35$
Percentage from total (%)	$\dfrac{\$35}{\$150} \times 100\% = 23.3\%$

Step 1: Turn the discount percentage into a decimal.

Step 2: Calculate the discount amount.

Step 3: Subtract the discount amount from the original price.

Step 4: Calculate the percentage from the total amount.

MW3.1: Eldon bought a zip-up hoodie from a shop that offered a 25% discount. If the original price was $30, what is the price after the discount, and what is its percentage from the $150 that Eldon has?

Discount (% into decimal)		
Discount amount ($)		
Price after discount ($)		
Percentage from total (%)		

MW3.2: Eldon bought a jogger from a shop that offered a 15% discount. If the original price was $15, what is the price after the discount, and what is its percentage from the $150 that Eldon has?

Discount (% into decimal)		
Discount amount ($)		
Price after discount ($)		
Percentage from total (%)		

MW3.3: Eldon bought three polo shirts from a shop that offered a 10% discount. If the original price for the three shirts was $20, what is the price after the discount, and what is its percentage from the $150 that Eldon has?

Discount (% into decimal)		
Discount amount ($)		
Price after discount ($)		
Percentage from total (%)		

MW3.4: Eldon bought a baseball shirt from a shop that offered a 40% discount. If the original price for the shirt was $10, what is the price after the discount, and what is its percentage from the $150 that Eldon has?

Discount (% into decimal)		
Discount amount ($)		
Price after discount ($)		
Percentage from total (%)		

MW3.5: Eldon bought high-top sneakers from a shop that offered a 35% discount. If the original price was $100, what is the price after the discount, and what is its percentage from the $150 that Eldon has?

Discount (% into decimal)		
Discount amount ($)		
Price after discount ($)		
Percentage from total (%)		

MW3.6: Eldon bought a cap from a shop that offered a 50% discount. If the original price was $12, what is the price after the discount, and what is its percentage from the $150 that Eldon has?

Discount (% into decimal)		
Discount amount ($)		
Price after discount ($)		
Percentage from total (%)		

MW3.7: Fill out the amounts and their percentages for all the items Eldon bought in MW3.1 to 3.6. How much total did he spend? What is the overall percentage of what he paid to the $150 he had?

	Hoodie	Jogger	Polo shirts	Baseball shirt	Sneakers	Cap	**Total**
Amount ($)							
Percentage (%)							

MW3.8: After Eldon bought the items in MW3.1 to MW3.6, how much money is left from his original $150? What is the percentage of the remaining money from what he originally had?

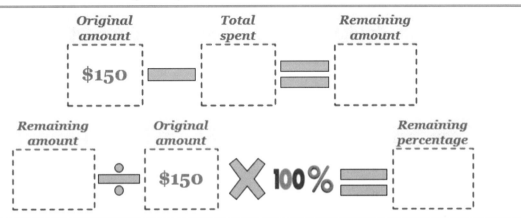

MW3.9: What is the fraction of shirts from all the items Eldon has bought? What is the corresponding percentage of that fraction?

(**Hint**: Calculate the number of shirts, including the 3 polo shirts and the baseball shirt, and divide them by the total number of items Eldon has bought.)

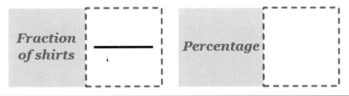

MW3.10: Compare the percentage of the number of shirts from the total number of items bought to the percentage of money spent on shirts from the total money spent. Which one is bigger?

Percentage of number of shirts   *Percentage of money spent on shirts*

(4) Pie Charts Discovery

A pie chart is a way to represent the data in a circular graph. The slices of the pie show how different pieces of information relate to the whole. Each slice has a different size depending on how big that information is.

Slices of a pie chart are usually presented in different colours with labels near each slice to tell you what it represents. Pie charts help you understand data quickly and see which part is bigger or smaller.

Example

Imagine you asked your classmates about their favourite ice cream flavours. You can create a pie chart to show the results. Suppose that you have 30 students in your classroom, and the results come like this:

Vanilla: 5

Chocolate: 10

Cookie: 8

Strawberry: 7

You can present this information in a pie chart by drawing a circle representing your classmates' ice cream preferences. The circle will be divided into slices representing the different flavours. Since 10 of your classmates like chocolate, the chocolate slice would be the biggest, whereas the vanilla slice would be the smallest. Near each slice, you will write the name of the ice cream flavour it represents. You can colour each slice differently to make it easy to see the portions of the pie chart. You can add the number of students who like each flavour or their percentages.

When you look at the pie chart, you see that chocolate is the most popular flavour among your classmates because its slice is the biggest. You can also tell that the second favourite is the cookie, followed by strawberry, and finally, the vanilla flavour.

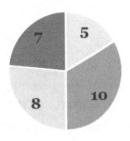

Vanilla ■ Chocolate ▪ Cookie ■ Strawberry

You could present the data using percentages instead of numbers. To do that, you first need to convert the numbers into fractions and then convert the fractions into percentages.

	Number	Fraction	Percentage
Vanilla	5	5/30	17%
Chocolate	10	10/30	33%
Cookie	8	8/30	27%
Strawberry	7	7/30	23%

Presenting the percentages on a pie chart makes it easy for anyone to identify the portions. When you look at the pie chart, you can see that 33% of your classmates like chocolate-flavoured ice cream. Cookie flavour came in second place with 27%, followed by strawberry flavour with 23%, and finally, 17% like the vanilla flavour.

Classmates ice cream flavour preferences

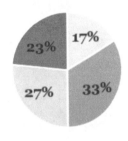

Vanilla ■ Chocolate ▪ Cookie ■ Strawberry

A pie chart is a fantastic way to show information in a colourful and easy-to-understand way. It helps you see immediately which category if the biggest or smallest. Eldon and Kayla used their pie chart skills to create a monthly budget, which greatly helped them save money!

Mental workout

Popcorn flavour preferences!

Eldon invited his best friends to watch a movie at his home. He wanted to prepare popcorn for them. He asked his friends what popcorn flavour they prefer. Help Eldon label the pie chart slices using the percentage of his friends who like each type of popcorn flavour.

Example

Label the slices based on the preferences of **12 best friends** of Eldon:

Popcorn flavour	Number	Percentage
Butter	5	$= \dfrac{5}{12} \times 100\% = 41\%$
Plain	3	$= \dfrac{3}{12} \times 100\% = 25\%$
Caramel	2	$= \dfrac{2}{12} \times 100\% = 17\%$
Cheese	2	$= \dfrac{2}{12} \times 100\% = 17\%$

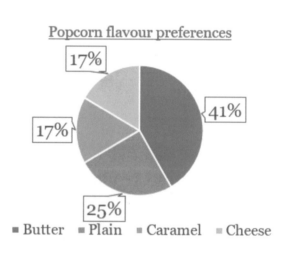

Step 1: Turn the number into a fraction of the total number.

Step 2: Convert the fraction into a percentage.

Step 3: Look at the legend to identify the slices.

Step 3: Write the percentage of each slice.

MW4.1: Label the slices based on the preferences of **12 best friends** of Eldon:

Popcorn flavour	Number	Percentage
Butter	3	
Plain	5	
Caramel	1	
Cheese	3	

Popcorn flavour preferences

- Butter - Plain - Caramel - Cheese

MW4.2: Label the slices based on the preferences of **12 best friends** of Eldon:

Popcorn flavour	Number	Percentage
Butter	1	
Plain	4	
Caramel	2	
Cheese	5	

Popcorn flavour preferences

- Butter - Plain - Caramel - Cheese

MW4.3: Label the slices based on the preferences of **12 best friends** of Eldon:

Popcorn flavour	Number	Percentage
Butter	3	
Plain	3	
Caramel	5	
Cheese	1	

Popcorn flavour preferences

- Butter - Plain - Caramel - Cheese

MW4.4: Label the slices based on the preferences of **15 best friends** of Eldon:

Popcorn flavour	Number	Percentage
Butter	6	
Plain	4	
Caramel	3	
Cheese	2	

Popcorn flavour preferences

■ Butter ■ Plain ■ Caramel ■ Cheese

MW4.5: Label the slices based on the preferences of **15 best friends** of Eldon:

Popcorn flavour	Number	Percentage
Butter	3	
Plain	6	
Caramel	2	
Cheese	4	

Popcorn flavour preferences

■ Butter ■ Plain ■ Caramel ■ Cheese

MW4.6: Label the slices based on the preferences of **15 best friends** of Eldon:

Popcorn flavour	Number	Percentage
Butter	4	
Plain	6	
Caramel	1	
Cheese	4	

Popcorn flavour preferences

■ Butter ■ Plain ■ Caramel ■ Cheese

MW4.7: Label the slices based on the preferences of 18 best friends of Eldon:

Popcorn flavour	Number	Percentage
Butter	6	
Plain	5	
Caramel	2	
Cheese	5	

Popcorn flavour preferences

■ Butter ■ Plain ■ Caramel ■ Cheese

MW4.8: Label the slices based on the preferences of 18 best friends of Eldon:

Popcorn flavour	Number	Percentage
Butter	4	
Plain	6	
Caramel	5	
Cheese	3	

Popcorn flavour preferences

■ Butter ■ Plain ■ Caramel ■ Cheese

MW4.9: Label the slices based on the preferences of 18 best friends of Eldon:

Popcorn flavour	Number	Percentage
Butter	2	
Plain	3	
Caramel	7	
Cheese	6	

Popcorn flavour preferences

■ Butter ■ Plain ■ Caramel ■ Cheese

(5) Budgeting Basics

A budget is a plan for spending and saving your money. By comparing the money coming in and going out, you can see what you can afford to spend, where you can save, and how long it takes you to save enough money for a particular goal.

Before you can start preparing your own budget or help others plan their spending and savings, you need to get familiar with the parts that form a budget:

1. Income

Income is the money you receive for doing something. Imagine you have a lemonade stand, and people are paying you for a glass of lemonade. The money you receive is your **income** from the lemon stand.

Your income could come from different sources, such as:

a) Allowance from your parents.

b) The money you earn from doing chores in your neighbourhood.

c) The money you receive from selling something.

d) The money paid to you for doing part-time work.

e) Cash gifts you receive on your birthday, Christmas, or other occasions.

When you grow up, the payment you receive from your job is your income. If you open your own business, the money you make from that business is your income. Some people earn money from investing in stocks or real estate; when these investments make money, they earn income.

2. Needs and wants

Needs are things that you must have to live and stay safe. They are essential for you, such as:

a) Food: You need food to stay alive and have energy.

b) Water: You need water to keep your body hydrated.

c) Home: You need a home to shelter you.

d) Clothing: Clothes protect your body from the weather.

e) Education: You need to learn to prepare for the future.

f) Health: You need to stay healthy to function correctly.

Wants are things you desire or wish for, but you do not need them to survive. They are nice to have, but you live without them, such as:

a) Toys and games: Fun, but you can live without them.

b) Chocolate: Tasty, but you won't get sick without them.

c) Ice creams: Awesome, but you survive without them.

d) Fancy clothing: Nice, but not necessary for basic living.

e) Vacations: Exciting, but life continues without them.

Understanding the difference between needs and wants is important because it helps you choose how to spend your money. It would be best to prioritize your needs before spending on your wants.

3. Saving goals

➤ Decide what you want to save money for. It could be a new video game, a bike, or a fun trip.

➤ Figure out how much money you will need to reach your goal.

➤ Plan how much to save. Divide your goal amount by how many weeks or months you want to save for.

The 50/30/20 rule

This Rule helps you learn how to use your money wisely. Think of your income, such as your monthly allowance, as a pie. Now divide that pie into three slices:

1. The needs slice (50%): This is the biggest slice because it includes important things for your everyday life.

2. The wants slice (30%): This slice is smaller than the needs slice because it includes things that are nice to have but aren't necessary for survival.

3. The savings slice (20%): This slice is your savings jar. 20% of your income goes into this jar to save for your goals.

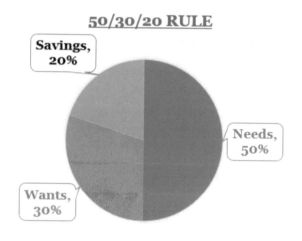

The 50/30/20 Rule makes sure that you have enough money for important stuff (the needs slice), enjoy some fun stuff (the wants slice), and still save up for your goals (the savings slice).

Example

Let's say you have a weekly allowance of $20, and your goal is to buy a bike that costs $140. You can use the 50/30/20 Rule to save enough money to buy the bike.

Step 1 – Income: Your income is the allowance you receive, which is $20 weekly.

Step 2 - Identify your needs: things you really need, like buying lunch at school and school supplies. 50% of your income is allocated for needs, therefore:

$$Needs = 50\% \times \$20 = 0.50 \times \$20 = \$10$$

Step 3 - Identify your wants: things you will get for fun, like buying a game or toy, a treat, or going to a movie. 30% of your income is allocated for wants, therefore:

$$Wants = 30\% \times \$20 = 0.30 \times \$20 = \$6$$

Step 4 – Set your savings goal: Your goal is to buy a bike that costs $140. 20% of your income is allocated for savings, therefore:

$$Savings = 20\% \times \$20 = 0.20 \times \$20 = \$4$$

Now you have your budget ready, you know that your $20 allowance is divided into:

1. $10 for important stuff you need, like lunch and school supplies.

2. $6 for fun things you want, like buying a game, a treat, or a movie ticket.

3. $4 to save up for your goal of buying a bike.

You can calculate when you can buy the bike by dividing the price of the bike by your weekly savings:

$$Weeks\ needed\ to\ save\ for\ a\ bike$$
$$= \frac{\$140}{\$4} = 35\ weeks$$

Therefore, you will have enough money to buy the bike after **35 weeks**, or approximately **9 months**.

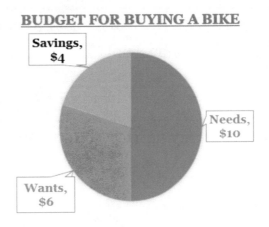

BUDGET FOR BUYING A BIKE

Savings, $4

Needs, $10

Wants, $6

Using the 50/30/20 Rule, you learn to be responsible with your money. You are ensuring you have what you need, enjoying some fun stuff, and saving up for an exciting goal. It is an intelligent way to manage your money!

Mental workout

Kayla prepares her first budget!

Kayla wanted to take care of her monthly expenses and asked her parents for a monthly allowance. However, her parents asked her how much she thinks her allowance should be. Luckily, Kayla knew about the **50/30/20 Rule** and decided to use it to calculate how much her monthly allowance should be. Help Kayla determine the allowance amount that would cover her monthly needs and allow her to enjoy some of her wants while saving for her future goals.

Kayla identifies her wants and needs:

MW5.1: Is buying a snack at school a need or a want?

| Needs | *or* | Wants |

MW5.2: Is buying an ice cream after school a need or a want?

| Needs | *or* | Wants |

MW5.3: Is buying stationary for school a need or a want?

| Needs | *or* | Wants |

MW5.4: Is buying a new dress once every three months a need or a want?

| Needs | *or* | Wants |

MW5.5: Is buying a new shoe once every six months a need or a want?

| Needs | *or* | Wants |

MW5.6: Is buying a new book once every month a need or a want?

| Needs | *or* | Wants |

MW5.7: Is buying medication a need or a want?

| Needs | *or* | Wants |

MW5.8: Is buying a video game once every 3 months a need or a want?

| Needs | *or* | Wants |

MW5.9: Is buying a hand sanitizer once every month a need or a want?

| Needs | *or* | Wants |

MW5.10: Is going on a trip once every six months a need or a want?

| Needs | *or* | Wants |

MW5.11: Is buying a birthday gift for Kayla's friends once every three months a need or a want?

| Needs | *or* | Wants |

MW5.12: Is buying chocolate a need or a want?

| Needs | *or* | Wants |

MW5.13: Is paying a monthly subscription to the gym a need or a want?

| Needs | *or* | Wants |

MW5.14: Is buying tickets for movies a need or a want?

| Needs | *or* | Wants |

MW5.15: Is buying a toothbrush once every six months a need or a want?

| Needs | *or* | Wants |

MW5.16: Help Kayla fill in the costs of her wants and needs in a table:

		Cost ($/month)	Needs	Wants
1	Snack at school	$60/month (20 snacks per month)		
2	Ice cream	$8/month (4 ice creams per month)		
3	Stationary for school	$4/month		
4	New dress	$25/month (A new dress costs $75 once every 3 months)		
5	New shoes	$10/month (A new shoe costs $60 once every 6 months)		
6	Books	$10/month		
7	Medication	$8/month		
8	Video game	$10/month (A video game costs $60 once every 6 months)		
9	Hand sanitizer	$4/month		
10	Trips	$5/month (A trip costs $30 once every 6 months)		
11	Birthday gifts	$10 (A birthday gift costs $30 once every 3 months)		
12	Chocolate	$8 (4 chocolate bars per month)		
13	Gym subscription	$12		
14	Movie ticket	$5 (A movie ticket costs $15 once every 3 months)		
15	Toothbrush	$2 (A new toothbrush costs $12 once every 6 months)		
	Total ($/month)			

MW5.17: What is the total of Kayla's needs per month?

(**Hint:** fill in the costs under Needs or Wants in the table and sum up the Needs total) $

MW5.18: What monthly allowance should Kayla ask her parents for?

(**Hint:** following the 50/30/20 Rule, we know that Needs are 50% of the income, so the allowance should be 2 x Needs) $

MW5.19: What is the monthly amount Kayla can spend on her Wants?

(**Hint:** following the 50/30/20 Rule, we know that Wants are 30% of the income, so the Wants amount should be 0.3 x Allowance) $

MW5.20: How much would Kayla save every month?

(**Hint:** following the 50/30/20 Rule, we know that Savings are 20% of the income, so the Savings amount should be 0.2 x Allowance) $

MW5.21: Label the pie chart with the Needs, Wants, and Savings amounts.

(**Hint:** Use the value you got from MW5.17 to label the Needs, the value you got from MW5.19 to label the Wants, and the value you got from MW5.20 to label the Savings)

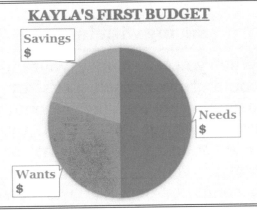

KAYLA'S FIRST BUDGET

Savings $

Needs $

Wants $

MW5.22: Kayla found that the amount allocated for her Wants in her first budget is lower than the Wants amount in her table. How could Kalya adjust her Wants to match the amount of Wants in her budget?

(**Hint:** you can reduce the Wants amount in the table in different ways, such as: a) remove some of the wants, b) reduce the quantities, such as 2 ice creams instead of 4, and c) increase the period needed to buy a want, such as you could reduce the monthly amount of a video game from $10 to $5 and increase the period from 6 to 12 months)

(6) Interest Unveiled

Interest is extra money that you earn when you save your money, or you pay when you borrow money. Imagine you have some money saved up in a savings account at the bank. When you leave your money there, the bank decides to give you a little extra money as a reward for keeping your money with them. This extra money is called interest.

Saving with interest	Borrowing with interest
When you save money, your money could grow by itself. Let's say you have $100 in a savings account at a bank, and the bank gives you 3% interest in one year. That means leaving your $100 in the savings account for one year will become $103. The longer you leave your money in the savings account, the more it grows.	When you borrow money, you pay them back with an interest. Let's say you borrowed $200 from a bank to buy a bike. The bank would lend you the money provided you pay them back with an interest of 5% per year. That means you will return $210 after one year. The longer the payback period, the higher the interest you pay.

An interest rate is a percentage that tells you how much extra money you can earn when you save or invest, or how much extra money you pay when you borrow. The interest rate can have different percentages. For example, the bank would offer you a low interest rate for your savings account, such as 2%, whereas it would charge you a higher interest when you take a loan. Credit card providers charge a very high interest if you borrow money using a credit card. An interest could be simple or compound:

Simple interest	Compound interest
Let's say you start with $100 in your savings account. This is your original money. The bank tells you they will give you a simple yearly interest of 5%. If you decide to withdraw your money after two years, your money will be:	If you start with $100 in your savings account, and the bank tells you they will give you a compound yearly interest of 5%. If you decide to withdraw your money after two years, your money will be:

Interest for the first year
$$= 0.05 \times \$100 = \$5$$

Interest for the second year
$$= 0.05 \times \$100 = \$5$$

Your money after two years
$$= \$100 + \$5 + \$5$$
$$= \$110$$

Interest for the first year
$$= 0.05 \times \$100 = \$5$$

Interest for the second year
$$= 0.05 \times \$105 = \$5.25$$

Your money after two years
$$= \$100 + \$5 + \$5.25$$
$$= \$110.25$$

That is, the simple interest is applied to the original amount every year. After the first year, you will have $5 interest. After the second year, you will have another $5 interest, making your total money $110. With simple interest, your money grows by the same amount each year.	That is, the interest you earn in the first year is added to your original amount. The $5 interest is added (compounded) to the original amount, making it $105. In the second year, the 5% interest is applied to the $105, not the original $100, making your total $110.25.

Simple interest is like a one-time bonus, whereas **compound interest** is like a bonus that keeps growing like a snowball that gets bigger as it rolls downhill.

Mental workout

Eldon's first savings account!

After learning the 50/30/20 Rule, Eldon started to save money for his future goals. Eldon realized that putting his savings in a savings account would grow his money over time. To maximize the potential growth of his money, Eldon started comparing savings account offers from several banks. Help Eldon select the best offer to maximize his earnings if he starts with $100.

MW6.1: Offer 1 - a simple interest rate of 2% every 6 months. How much would Eldon's original $100 be after 1 year?

Interest cycles in 1 year	= 12 months/6 months = 2 cycles
Interest earned in 1 year	= Interest cycles × Original amount × interest rate = 2 cycles × $100 × 0.02 = $4
Eldon's money in 1 year	= Original amount + Interest earned = $100 + $4 = $104

MW6.2: Offer 2 - offers a simple interest rate of 1% every 3 months. How much would Eldon's original $100 be after 1 year?

Interest cycles in 1 year	
Interest earned in 1 year	
Eldon's money in 1 year	

MW6.3: **Offer 3 -** a simple interest rate of 1.5% every 4 months. How much would Eldon's original $100 be after 1 year?

Interest cycles in 1 year	
Interest earned in 1 year	
Eldon's money in 1 year	

MW6.4: **Offer 4 -** offers a simple interest rate of 2.5% every 8 months. How much would Eldon's original $100 be after 1 year?

Interest cycles in 1 year	
Interest earned in 1 year	
Eldon's money in 1 year	

MW6.5: **Offer 5 -** offers a simple interest rate of 3% every 9 months. How much would Eldon's original $100 be after 1 year?

Interest cycles in 1 year	
Interest earned in 1 year	
Eldon's money in 1 year	

MW6.6: **Offer 6 -** offers a simple interest rate of 3.5% every 12 months. How much would Eldon's original $100 be after 1 year?

Interest cycles in 1 year	
Interest earned in 1 year	
Eldon's money in 1 year	

MW6.7: **Offer 7 -** offers a simple interest rate of 0.5% every 1 month. How much would Eldon's original $100 be after 1 year?

Interest cycles in 1 year	
Interest earned in 1 year	
Eldon's money in 1 year	

MW6.8: **Offer 8** - offers a simple interest rate of 1% every 2 months. How much would Eldon's original $100 be after 1 year?

Interest cycles in 1 year	
Interest earned in 1 year	
Eldon's money in 1 year	

MW6.9: **Offer 9** - offers a simple interest rate of 1.5% every 3 months. How much would Eldon's original $100 be after 1 year?

Interest cycles in 1 year	
Interest earned in 1 year	
Eldon's money in 1 year	

MW6.10: **Offer 10** - offers a simple interest rate of 3.5% every 9 months. How much would Eldon's original $100 be after 1 year?

Interest cycles in 1 year	
Interest earned in 1 year	
Eldon's money in 1 year	

MW6.11: **Offer 11** - offers a simple interest rate of 3% every 4 months. How much would Eldon's original $100 be after 1 year?

Interest cycles in 1 year	
Interest earned in 1 year	
Eldon's money in 1 year	

MW6.12: Compare offers 1 to 11; which offer Eldon should select to maximize the interest earned on his original $100?

Best offer:	

After selecting the best-paying savings account from offers 1 to 11, Eldon went to the bank and deposited $100. He plans to withdraw his money after 1 year with the interest he carns. However, an email from the bank offered him a 5% compound interest yearly if he kept his money in the savings account for 5 years. Help Eldon calculate the amount of money he will receive after 5 years if he accepts the 5-year compound interest offer.

MW6.13	What will the original $100 be after 1 year?	= $100 + (0.05 × $100) = $105
MW6.14	What will the original $100 be after 2 years?	= $105 + (0.05 × $105) = $110.25
MW6.15	What will the original $100 be after 3 years?	
MW6.16	What will the original $100 be after 4 years?	
MW6.17	What will the original $100 be after 5 years?	
MW6.18	What is the total interest amount in 5 years? (**Hint**: subtract the amount of money Eldon receives after 5 years from the original amount of money)	
MW6.19	What is the percentage growth of Eldon's money in 5 years? (**Hint**: Divide the final amount Eldon receives after 5 years by the original amount and multiply the result by 100%)	

(7) The Science of Investing

Investing is like planting seeds to grow a money tree. Imagine having some extra money from savings from your allowance or birthday gifts. Instead of spending this money, you could do something clever and watch it grow. However, it would help to know what to invest in.

Choose what to invest in

You need to pick an investment opportunity that is known to be profitable. People usually invest in several options, such as:

(1) Stocks

Investing in stocks is like buying a tiny portion of a big company. Imagine a big company, like a famous video game company. This company sells its products to people and makes a profit. When you buy a stock in this company, you become a part owner. As the company makes a profit, they share some of it with those who own their stock. The value of your share goes up and down based on how much money the company is making.

Stock Market

When you invest in stocks, you own a piece of a company. You become a mini business owner holding shares in the company. However, there is a risk of losing money if the company does not do well. You can sell your shares when you decide. If the value of the shares when you sell is higher than the original value, you make a profit; if the share's value is less than the original value, you make a loss.

(2) Bonds

Bonds are like lending your money to a company or the government. They promise to pay back your money plus interest after a specific time. It's like a loan that you give, and it's usually less risky than stocks. The cool part is that while they have your money, they also pay you interest for letting them use your money.

(3) Real Estate

Real estate investing is like buying or owning properties, such as houses, apartments, or lands, to generate income. There are two main ways to make money from these properties. First, you can rent them to people who need a place to live or work; they pay you a monthly rent, which becomes your income. Second, you can sell the property after some time when it becomes more valuable. Real estate investing is a great way to build wealth; however, it comes with risks, such as decreased property value and dealing with difficult tenants.

(4) Mutual funds

These are a mix of different investments, such as stocks, bonds, and real estate, combined in one bundle. The idea is to spread the risk and not rely on just one investment to grow your money. This way, if one investment is not doing well, you still can earn money from the other investments. Therefore, the risk of losing money in a mutual fund is much lower than investing in stocks.

Mental workout

Kayla's first investment!

After learning about different investment opportunities, Kayla decided to use her savings to invest in stocks. She did her research and found a well-established high-tech company. The company is listed in the stock market. Kayla asked her parents to open an investing account for her on a platform that allows her to buy and sell stocks.

Kayla wants to invest $100 in the high-tech company. The share price offered on the stocks platform for this company is $10 per share.

MW7.1: How many shares can Kalya buy with her $100?

Number of shares $= \dfrac{\text{Original amount (\$)}}{\text{Share price (\$)}} = \dfrac{\$100}{\$10} = $ ☐

MW7.2: How much will Kayla's original $100 be after 1 month if the share price becomes $10.5 per share?

Investment value after 1 month

Number of shares × Share price ($)

$=$ ☐ $\times$ ☐ $=$ ☐

MW7.3: How much did Kayla make after 1 month?

Current value ($) − Originalvalue ($)

Profit/loss $=$ ☐ $-$ ☐ $=$ ☐

MW7.4: Did Kayla make a profit or loss after 1 month?

Profit/loss

☐ Profit ☐ Loss

(Hint: Check the answer of MW7.3; if the value you got is positive, it indicates a profit; if the value you got is negative, it indicates a loss.)

MW7.5: How much will Kayla's original $100 be after 2 months if the share price becomes $9.5 per share?

Investment value after 2 months	=	Number of shares × Share price ($)		
	=	[ ]	× [ ]	= [ ]

MW7.6: How much did Kayla make after 2 months?

Profit/loss	=	Current value ($) − Originalvalue ($)		
	=	[ ]	− [ ]	= [ ]

MW7.7: Did Kayla make a profit or loss after 2 months?

Profit/loss	[Profit]	[Loss]

MW7.8: How much will Kayla's original $100 be after 3 months if the share price becomes $11 per share?

Investment value after 3 months	=	Number of shares × Share price ($)		
	=	[ ]	× [ ]	= [ ]

MW7.9: How much did Kayla make after 3 months?

Profit/loss	=	Current value ($) − Originalvalue ($)		
	=	[ ]	− [ ]	= [ ]

MW7.10: Did Kayla make a profit or loss after 3 months?

Profit/loss	[Profit]	[Loss]

MW7.11: What is the percentage growth in Kayla's money if she sells her shares after 3 months?

$$\% \text{ growth} = \frac{\text{Current value (\$)}}{\text{Original value (\$)}} \times 100\% = \boxed{}$$

(8) Tax Simplified

Tax is like a portion of your money you give to the government to help pay for things that benefit everyone in your country. The government collects taxes from individuals and businesses to pay for shared services, such as schools, hospitals, roads, and parks.

There are different types of taxes with different percentages. The tax you pay is based on how much you earn and how much you spend.

Income tax

Income could be earned from different sources, such as a salary from a regular job or a profit from an investment. The government collects a percentage of that income. People who make more money pay a higher percentage of their income in taxes. Adults fill out tax forms yearly to report their income and calculate how much tax they owe.

The government collects taxes from every adult's paycheck based on their income. For example, the government would collect 30% of earnings from an adult whose yearly income is more than $100,000, whereas the percentage collected from an adult whose annual income is less than $40,000 would be around 15%. By the end of the year, the government receives the tax forms and decides if they have deducted the correct tax amounts; if the deductions are higher, they issue a tax return.

Sales tax

Sales is the extra money you pay when you buy things. When you shop for groceries, clothes, toys, or electronics, you will pay the original price plus a sales tax. For example, if you buy a video game for $10 and the sales tax is 10%, you will end up paying $11 at the cashier. That additional $1 is a sales tax. The store where you buy the item collects tax for the government. Sales tax varies from place to place; different cities may have different rates.

Property tax

Property tax is a fee that people who own a property pay to their local government. The property could be a home, a land, or a building. The government figures out how much the property is worth. The value is based on several factors, such as the size, location, and what it is used for. The government collects a percentage of that value as property tax. This percentage varies from city to city, depending on the laws and regulations.

Taxes are like dues we pay to the government for the benefit of our community and country. The government uses the taxes to build and maintain schools, hospitals, parks, public buildings and other essential things that we need in our daily lives. People who earn more contribute a little more to help those who earn less.

Mental workout

Eldon becomes a financial advisor!

After learning about investment, interest, and tax, Eldon decided to set a plan for his future. He wants to study finance and become a financial advisor! Eldon also considered having a secondary income from an investment. Knowing that not all he earns would end up in his pocket since he will have to pay taxes, he started calculating his net income after tax!

Eldon expects to receive a starting salary of $4,000 per month when he works as a financial advisor. He also plans to invest in real estate and expects a profit of $500 per month from this investment. The income tax in his city is divided into brackets as follows:

	Income tax bracket ($)	Tax rate (%)
Tax bracket 1	$0 to $11,000	11%
Tax bracket 2	$11,000 - $45,000	16%
Tax bracket 3	$45,000 - $95,000	28%
Tax bracket 4	$95,000 - $182,000	30%

It means that, for income up to $11,000, Eldon will pay a tax rate of 11%. For income between $11,000 and $45,000, Eldon will pay a tax rate of 16%, and so on.

MW8.1: What will be Eldon's total income per month?

Total monthly income	= Salary income + Investment profit = $4,000 + $500 = $4500

MW8.2: What will be Eldon's total income per year?

Total yearly income	= Total monthly income × 12 = $\boxed{}$

MW8.3: How much of Eldon's total yearly income is under tax bracket 1?

Income under bracket 1	(Hint: Eldon's total yearly income is more than the upper limit of bracket 1; therefore, his income below $11,000 goes under bracket 1.) = Bracket 1 Upper limit − Bracket 1 lower limit = \$11,000 − \$0 = $\boxed{}$

MW8.4: How much tax will Eldon pay under tax bracket 1?

Tax under bracket 1	(Hint: Multiply the yearly income that falls under bracket 1, which is $11,000, by the bracket 1 tax rate.) = Income under bracket 1 × Bracket 1 tax rate = $\boxed{}$ × 0.11 = $\boxed{}$

MW8.5: How much of Eldon's total yearly income is under tax bracket 2?

Income under bracket 2	(Hint: Eldon's total yearly income is more than the upper limit of bracket 2; therefore, his income higher than $11,000 and lower than $45,000 goes under bracket 2.) = Bracket 2 Upper limit − Bracket 2 lower limit = \$45,000 − $\boxed{}$ = $\boxed{}$

MW8.6: How much tax will Eldon pay under tax bracket 2?

Tax under bracket 2

(Hint: Multiply the yearly income that falls under bracket 2, which is the MW8.5 answer, by the bracket 2 tax rate.)

= Income under bracket 2 × Bracket 2 tax rate

$$= \boxed{} \times 0.16 = \boxed{}$$

MW8.7: How much of Eldon's total yearly income is under tax bracket 3?

Income under bracket 3

(Hint: Eldon's total yearly income is less than the upper limit of bracket 3; therefore, his income higher than $45,000 and lower than $95,000 goes under bracket 3.)

= Total yearly income − Bracket 3 lower limit

$$= \$54{,}000 - \boxed{} = \boxed{}$$

MW8.8: How much tax will Eldon pay under tax bracket 3?

Tax under bracket 3

(Hint: Multiply the yearly income that falls under bracket 3, which is the MW8.7 answer, by the bracket 3 tax rate.)

= Income under bracket 3 × Bracket 3 tax rate

$$= \boxed{} \times 0.28 = \boxed{}$$

MW8.9: How much of Eldon's total yearly income is under tax bracket 4?

Income under bracket 4

(Hint: Eldon's total yearly income is less than the lower limit of bracket 4; therefore, he has no income under bracket 4.)

$$= \boxed{}$$

MW8.10: How much tax will Eldon pay under tax bracket 4?

Tax under bracket 4

(Hint: Eldon has no income under tax bracket 4; therefore, he will not pay tax under this bracket.)

$$= \boxed{}$$

MW8.11: How much total tax will Eldon pay?

Total tax

(Hint: The total tax is the summation of the tax under each bracket.)

= Tax under bracket 1 + Tax under bracket 2

+Tax under bracket 2 + Tax under bracket 4

$$= \boxed{} + \boxed{} + \boxed{} + \boxed{}$$

$$= \boxed{}$$

MW8.12: What will be Eldon's net income after tax?

Net income after tax

(Hint: The net income after tax is the original income before tax (called the gross income) minus the tax.)

= Income before tax − Tax

$$= \$54,000 - \boxed{} = \boxed{}$$

MW8.13: What is the actual percentage of tax from Eldon's original income?

Effective tax rate

(Hint: The actual percentage (called the effective tax rate) is the amount of tax paid divided by the income before tax times 100%.)

$$= \frac{\text{Tax}}{\text{Income before tax}} \times 100\% = \boxed{}$$

(9) Mastering Number Sense

Number sense is like having a superpower that helps you work with numbers in your everyday life. A strong number sense enables you to solve a wide range of math problems more quickly. Here are a few examples of the superpowers number sense can give you:

Counting

Number sense starts with counting. You can develop your skills in counting, whether it is how many friends you have, how many balloons are in a party, how many days are left in a month, or how many pages are left in your book. Counting is the foundation of math; before you step into advanced math, you need to master counting!

Comparing

Using number sense, you can easily compare numbers and quantities. For example, you can tell that 10 is bigger than 5. This is super useful when you need to make choices, like picking a larger cake or buying a cheaper shirt. In math classes, you will always need to compare numbers to solve problems, such as finding the difference between two numbers or figuring out which fraction is bigger!

Adding and subtracting

You can use number sense to add and subtract numbers mentally. It is like solving puzzles with numbers. You use addition and subtraction in your daily life, such as figuring out how much allowance you have left, how many hours until you play a soccer game, or how many mental work problems you solved correctly. Adding and subtracting are powerful tools for solving all kinds of problems.

Estimating

Number sense helps you make educated guesses. For example, after a test, you can estimate what your mark will be. At the store, you can estimate how much your items will cost. You can estimate how long it will take you to walk to school. When you have a math problem, estimating can give you an idea of the answer!

Recognizing patterns

Number sense helps you recognize patterns in numbers. Finding patterns in numbers is like solving a fun puzzle. Imagine numbers as puzzle pieces; identifying patterns is like spotting the shapes that fit together. You can use patterns to predict what might happen next!

Mental workout

Number in a jar!

Eldon and Kayla went to a cool competition where they could use their pattern-recognizing skills for an opportunity to win a free video game. There were rows of jars with numbers; some had hidden numbers. Those who find the jar with a hidden number 99 can win the free video game. Follow the patterns with Eldon and Kayla to find the hidden numbers!

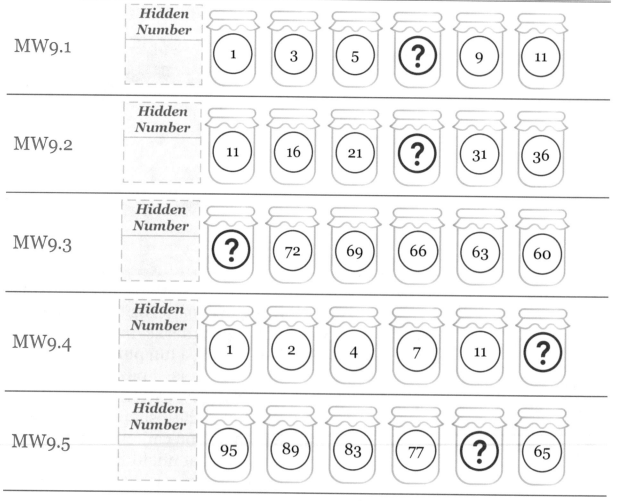

MW9.1 — Hidden Number: [ ] — 1, 3, 5, ?, 9, 11

MW9.2 — Hidden Number: [ ] — 11, 16, 21, ?, 31, 36

MW9.3 — Hidden Number: [ ] — ?, 72, 69, 66, 63, 60

MW9.4 — Hidden Number: [ ] — 1, 2, 4, 7, 11, ?

MW9.5 — Hidden Number: [ ] — 95, 89, 83, 77, ?, 65

MW9.6   Hidden Number   88   77   66   ?   44   33

MW9.7   Hidden Number   7   8   6   7   5   ?

MW9.8   Hidden Number   1   2   4   7   11   ?

MW9.9   Hidden Number   ?   98   96   93   89   84

MW9.10   Hidden Number   2   4   ?   16   32   64

MW9.11   Hidden Number   80   77   79   ?   78   75

MW9.12   Hidden Number   72   77   76   81   ?   85

MW9.13   In which jar did Elon and Kayla find the winning number 99?

Solutions

	MW1.1		MW1.2	
	Fraction A	Fraction B	Fraction A	Fraction B
Fraction	1/4	1/5	2/4	2/5
Equivalent fraction with common denominator	5/20	4/20	10/20	8/20
Which fraction is bigger?	Fraction A		Fraction A	

	MW1.3		MW1.4	
	Fraction A	Fraction B	Fraction A	Fraction B
Fraction	3/7	3/8	3/7	5/8
Equivalent fraction with common denominator	24/56	21/56	24/56	35/56
Which fraction is bigger?	Fraction A		Fraction B	

	MW1.5		MW1.6	
	Fraction A	Fraction B	Fraction A	Fraction B
Fraction	5/7	4/5	6/8	5/6
Equivalent fraction with common denominator	25/35	28/35	36/48	40/48
Which fraction is bigger?	Fraction B		Fraction B	

	MW1.7		MW1.8	
	Fraction A	Fraction B	Fraction A	Fraction B
Fraction	3/5	4/7	4/6	5/7
Equivalent fraction with common denominator	21/35	20/35	28/42	30/42
Which road is shorter?	Fraction B		Fraction A	

	MW2.1		MW2.2	
	Fraction	Winning Fraction	Fraction	Winning Fraction
Fraction of monkeys with bananas	1/6	2/3	3/9	2/3
Fractions with common denominators	1/6	4/6	3/9	6/9
Did Kayla win?	N		N	

	MW2.3		MW2.4	
	Fraction	Winning Fraction	Fraction	Winning Fraction
Fraction of monkeys with bananas	4/11	2/3	2/5	2/3
Fractions with common denominators	12/33	22/33	6/15	10/15
Did Kayla win?	N		N	

	MW2.5		MW2.6
	Fraction	Winning Fraction	Winning rounds
Fraction of monkeys with bananas	7/10	2/3	
Fractions with common denominators	21/30	20/30	• Round 5
Did Kayla win?	Y		

	Discount	Discount amount ($)	Price after discount ($)	Percentage from total (%)
MW3.1	25%=0.25	$7.50	$22.50	15.00%
MW3.2	15%=0.15	$2.25	$12.75	8.50%
MW3.3	11%=0.10	$2.00	$18.00	12.00%
MW3.4	40%=0.40	$4.00	$6.00	4.00%
MW3.5	35%=0.35	$35.00	$65.00	43.33%
MW3.6	50%=0.50	$6.00	$6.00	4.00%
MW3.7	Total amount spent: $130.25		Overall percentage: 86.83%	
MW3.8	Remaining amount: $19.75		Remaining percentage: 13.17%	
MW3.9	Fraction of shirts: 4/8		Percentage: 50.00%	
MW3.10	Percentage of shirts: 50.00%		Percentage of money spent on shirts: 16.00%	

	Butter	Plain	Caramel	Cheese
MW4.1	25%	42%	8%	25%
MW4.2	8%	33%	17%	42%
MW4.3	25%	25%	42%	8%
MW4.4	40%	27%	20%	13%
MW4.5	20%	40%	13%	27%
MW4.6	27%	40%	7%	27%
MW4.7	33%	28%	11%	28%
MW4.8	22%	33%	28%	17%
MW4.9	11%	17%	39%	33%

MW5.1	Needs	MW5.6	Needs	MW5.11	Wants
MW5.2	Wants	MW5.7	Needs	MW5.12	Wants
MW5.3	Needs	MW5.8	Wants	MW5.13	Needs
MW5.4	Wants	MW5.9	Needs	MW5.14	Wants
MW5.5	Needs	MW5.10	Wants	MW5.15	Needs

MW5.16

		Cost ($/month)	Needs	Wants
1	Snack at school	$60/month	$60	
2	Ice cream	$8/month		$8
3	Stationary for school	$4/month	$4	
4	New dress	$25/month		$25
5	New shoes	$10/month		$10
6	Books	$10/month	$10	
7	Medication	$8/month	$8	
8	Video game	$10/month		$10
9	Hand sanitizer	$4/month	$4	
10	Trips	$5/month		$5
11	Birthday gifts	$10		$10
12	Chocolate	$8		$8
13	Gym subscription	$12	$12	
14	Movie ticket	$5		$5
15	Toothbrush	$2	$2	
	Total ($/month)		$100	$81

MW5.17	Needs per month: $100	
MW5.18	Monthly allowance: $200	
MW5.19	Wants per month: $60	
MW5.20	Savings per month: $40	

MW5.21

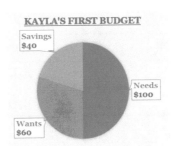

KAYLA'S FIRST BUDGET

Savings $40
Needs $100
Wants $60

MW5.22 — The wants amount in the table is $81, whereas the wants in Kalya's budget is $60. Therefore, Kayla should remove $21 from her monthly wants. For example, video game costs could be reduced from $10 to $5, and the period adjusted from 6 months to 12 months.

	Interest cycles in 1 year	Interest earned in 1 year ($)	Eldon's money in 1 year ($)
MW6.1	2	$4	$104
MW6.2	4	$4	$104
MW6.3	3	$4.5	$104.5
MW6.4	1.5	$3.75	103.75
MW6.5	1.33	$4	$104
MW6.6	1	$3.5	$103.5
MW6.7	12	$6	$106
MW6.8	6	$6	$106
MW6.9	4	$6	$106
MW6.10	1.33	$4.67	$104.67
MW6.11	3	$9	$109
MW6.12	Offer 11	MW6.13	$105
MW6.14	$110.25	MW6.15	$115.51
MW6.16	$120.78	MW6.17	$126.04
MW6.18	$26.04	MW6.19	126%
MW7.1	10	MW7.2	$105
MW7.3	$5	MW7.4	Profit
MW7.5	$95	MW7.6	-$5
MW7.7	Loss	MW7.8	$110
MW7.9	$10	MW7.10	Profit

MW8.1	$4,500	MW8.2	$54,000
MW8.3	$11,000	MW8.4	$1,210
MW8.5	$34,000	MW8.6	$5,440
MW8.7	$9,000	MW8.8	$2,520
MW8.9	$0	MW8.10	$0
MW8.11	$9,170	MW8.12	$44,830
MW8.13	16.98%		

MW9.1	7	MW9.2	26
MW9.3	75	MW9.4	16
MW9.5	71	MW9.6	55
MW9.7	6	MW9.8	16
MW9.9	99	MW9.10	8
MW9.11	76	MW9.12	80
MW9.13	The jar in MW9.9		

Future SmartMinds

Future ✚━✖÷═ Mathematician

www.futuresmartminds.com

Welcome to the **FutureSmartMinds** family!

Thank you for choosing "**Future Mathematician**". Your support means the world to us as we strive to develop young minds in STEM (Science, Technology, Engineering, and Mathematics) skills. We believe that learning should be engaging and fun, and "**Future Mathematician**" is designed to make math an exciting adventure for young learners.

Your feedback is incredibly valuable to us. If you have a moment, please consider sharing your thoughts and rating us on Amazon. Your input not only helps us improve but also guides other parents and educators in their quest for high-quality STEM resources.

Scan to Rate Us on Amazon

Thank you for your trust in **FutureSmartMinds**. Together, we're nurturing future mathematicians and fostering a love for learning in the minds of tomorrow. Happy learning!

Warm regards,

The **FutureSmartMinds** Team

www.futuresmartminds.com

Email: FutureSmartMindsKids@gmail.com

🅿 @futuresmartminds

f @futuresmartminds

📷 @ futuresmartminds

Scan to visit our website

Please check our other kids' **STEM** activities books!

Available on Amazon!

(Scan the QR code to visit Amazon store)

Introduce your child to the captivating world of engineering." This exceptional book is tailored for budding young minds, ages 7 to 12, and is brimming with astonishing STEM engineering experiments that ignite creativity and critical thinking.

Unleash Engineering Wonders: Engineering is all around us, but sometimes it can seem complex. "**Future Engineer**" bridges this gap by unveiling mind-blowing engineering experiments that use everyday household items, making engineering accessible, exciting, and hands-on. These experiments spark curiosity and develop analytical skills.

Available on Amazon!

(Scan the QR code to visit our Amazon store)

Prepare for an exciting journey into the world of science! Our book is designed to captivate young minds, ages 7 to 12, with engaging experiments that uncover the magic of scientific concepts. These experiments unravel unpredictable phenomena, demonstrating that science explains the unexplained.

Unlock the World of Science: Science is all around us, and we've crafted mind-blowing experiments using everyday household items to demystify its wonders. These activities nurture analytical skills, critical thinking, and curiosity in physics, biology, chemistry, space, and technology.

Available on Amazon!

(Scan the QR code to visit Amazon store)

Unleash Your Child's Potential with Artificial Intelligence (AI)! **"Future AI Expert,"** where the wonders of artificial intelligence unfold through 20 captivating activities. Designed for young minds aged 7-12, this book offers a thrilling introduction to AI, blending education with a whole lot of interactive fun.

20 Amazing AI Activities: Engage with a variety of projects, from AI-powered storytelling to problem-solving games, each designed to spark curiosity and encourage exploration.

Easy to Follow, Fun to Learn: With kid-friendly instructions, the complex world of AI becomes an exciting playground for young minds.

Available on Amazon!

(Scan the QR code to visit Amazon store)

Prepare to embark on an exciting journey where the joy of **cooking** meets the wonder of **science**! This vibrant cookbook is packed with **25 delicious cooking experiments** crafted for young chefs, aged 7 to 12, offering diverse hands-on experiments across five captivating sections: Bake, Grill, Boil, Fry, and Desserts.

Interactive Learning Experience: With step-by-step instructions, ingredient lists, and required equipment for each cooking experiment, **'Future Chef'** transforms the kitchen into a vivid laboratory. Through vibrant illustrations, scientific principles come alive, ensuring that each recipe is an engaging exploration of culinary science.

Made in the USA
Columbia, SC
20 July 2024

39014013R00041